The Threat to Corporate Growth

Photograph by Alfred Eisenstaedt

James J. Needham

The Threat to Corporate Growth

by James J. Needham

Introduction by
William McChesney Martin, Jr.

Written for and published by Girard Bank • February, 1974

James J. Needham is Chairman of the New York Stock Exchange, the first full time Chairman in its history.

Mr. Needham's ascent on Wall Street spans three decades. He began as a part-time messenger delivering securities for the old Continental Bank. He graduated from St. John's University in Brooklyn, New York with a Bachelor of Business Administration degree in 1951, after having also attended Cornell University. In 1972 his alma mater awarded him an honorary Doctor of Laws degree.

Mr. Needham has been closely associated with the New York accounting and business community throughout his professional career. In 1969, he was appointed a member of the Securities and Exchange Commission, a post he held until becoming Chairman of the New York Stock Exchange in 1972.

A noted speaker and an internationally recognized authority on the investment markets, Mr. Needham was elected to serve as Vice President of The Federation Internationale des Bourses de Valeurs, the International Federation of Stock Exchanges.

Mr. Needham is a member of the New York Chamber of Commerce, The Bond Club of New York, New York University Finance Club, Capitol Hill Club. He is a member of The Financial Accounting Standards Advisory Council and a Director of the Downtown-Lower Manhattan Association.

A Navy veteran, Mr. Needham was born in Woodhaven, New York in 1926. He and his wife have three sons and two daughters.

"The Threat to Corporate Growth" is printed on recycled paper.
Copyright 1974 by The Girard Company.
Library of Congress Catalog Number 74-77248.
Printed in the United States of America.

Girard Essays

THE QUALITY OF LIFE

James A. Michener

1970

AN URBAN PLANET?

Barbara Ward

1971

PAUL NADLER WRITES ABOUT BANKING

Dr. Paul Nadler

1972

THE NEW MAJORITY

Patrick J. Buchanan

1973

THE THREAT TO CORPORATE GROWTH

James J. Needham

1974

*"The Quality of Life," "An Urban Planet?"
and "Paul Nadler Writes About Banking"
are out of print.*

INTRODUCTION

In this timely and constructive essay on the threat to corporate growth, the Chairman of the Board of the New York Stock Exchange, James J. Needham, points up very well the role of the auction market in raising capital to finance our economy. I fully concur in his analysis and he rightly brings to our attention how serious the threat to corporate growth may be if this market continues to be fragmented and the role of the organized exchange is diminished.

The main thrust of the report on the securities markets, which I submitted to the Board of Governors of the New York Stock Exchange at their request on August 5, 1971, was the importance of creating a national exchange market system to provide an auction market, regardless of geographic location, for each security qualified for listing. In addition, reorganization of the Board of Governors of the New York Stock Exchange was proposed in order to reflect in its governance the needs of a modern corporation serving the public. The latter recommendation has been carried out and significant progress is now being made to implement the former.

I am basically optimistic. The problems we face in the securities industry are not insuperable, but the financing requirements of corporations over the next several years will run into the billions and the trillions of dollars and our markets will be strained to their limits. All of us recognize the need for change. However, it is imperative that in any restructuring of our markets we make improvements and not undermine and weaken a market such as the auction market which has provided maximum opportunity for public buyers and sellers to effect trades directly through their agents . . . as opposed to a market in which the public must trade with dealers trading for their own account. The basic question now is whether this market will gradually become one in which the public must perforce deal almost exclusively with professionals as in so many European markets.

It is easy to see ghosts and to raise unjustifiable fears whenever change in a time honored practice is proposed, but our markets have been so clearly the best in the world that it behooves us to think through all our moves to be sure we are not impairing their vitality. Ultimately, I am convinced, we will develop a Federal Securities System patterned after the one we have for banking in the Federal Reserve System, and perhaps there will be an industry-wide board of all the exchanges linked together and acting under the supervision of the Securities and Exchange Commission.

I fully endorse the discussion of the auction market in this essay and think all corporate executives who are concerned about their securities would do well to study it and support such a market.

William McChesney Martin, Jr.

President, New York Stock Exchange
1938-1941
Chairman, Federal Reserve Board
1951-1970

FOREWORD

A threat to corporate growth?

The American business community has faced threats before, and has shown that it can take perfectly good care of itself, thank you. Economic crises, labor strife, material shortages, restrictive legislation, foreign competition—Corporate America has been through them all and has emerged from each test stronger than before.

True enough. My admiration for the strength, ingenuity and resiliency of our nation's business community is second to none.

My concern stems from the fact that it is necessary to recognize a threat in order to be able to deal with it. And my thesis is that Corporate America today is facing a grave threat to its continued growth—and does *not* recognize it.

James J. Needham

Contents

THE THREAT TO CORPORATE GROWTH

Each year, half a million people step out on the Visitor's Gallery overlooking the trading floor of the New York Stock Exchange. The scene below is a fascinating, seemingly aimless jumble of movement. Hundreds of figures scurry this way and that—brokers, clerks, reporters, pages—bringing in and matching the bulk of some 100,000 orders to buy and sell securities that flow into the exchange every day.

High above the trading floor—more constant movement—as the huge ticker tape reports on the activity below, recording the minute-by-minute changes in stock values, keeping tabs on the rising and declining fortunes of 1,600 of the world's largest corporate enterprises.

This is the hub of America's capitalist system. This is the market where 20 billion shares of corporate stock can be traded, and 4 billion shares are traded each year—more often than not at the same price or at a price just 12½¢ higher or lower than the preceding sale in the same stock. This market in motion is, in fact, a vast pool of supply and demand, where agents for buyers and sellers transfer millions of dollars in securities, carrying out the investment decisions—many of them made hundreds or thousands of miles away just a few moments earlier—that determine corporate values.

In the most meaningful sense, this is an evaluat-

growing directly or indirectly out of the energy crisis to make even the widest-ranging projections of future needs instantly obsolete.

It is also worth noting that government today is not merely the biggest U.S. borrower—it also enjoys, in many instances, privileges not available to borrowers in the private sector. The borrowing agencies, by way of burgeoning Federal credit programs, are often free from the scrutiny of elected public officials and, in effect, able to set their own borrowing standards and disciplines.

Thus far, the U.S. capital markets have been able to meet the combined demands of the private and public sectors. But the markets' ability to continue channeling the billions of dollars needed every year to fuel corporate expansion will hinge on the ability of the private sector itself to earn and maintain public confidence. We can expect the most reliable indicator of public confidence to be—as it has been over the past generation—the extent of voluntary public participation in the market. And voluntary public participation, in turn, will depend heavily on whether or not the U.S. securities markets continue to exhibit the three key characteristics which make them unique: sensitivity, stability, and liquidity.

Many, perhaps most, corporate executives tend to overlook the mutually beneficial relationship between a high degree of direct, voluntary public participation in the securities markets and a corporation's ability to finance its own growth. I have heard

4

one chief executive officer after another declare that the securities markets are really no more than a luxury, that corporate growth and expansion are most effectively financed through retained earnings. And, indeed last year, U.S. corporations plowed back 60% of earnings into new plant and equipment, research and development and all of the increasingly costly improvements which contribute to corporate excellence and help determine corporate competitiveness.

The availability of retained earnings has, in fact, become so much a part of the corporate way of life in this country, that many corporate executives seem to think that a profitable operation guarantees the ability to reinvest a high proportion of earnings.

The fact is that retained earnings are available to many profitable corporations largely because stockholders are willing to forego immediate high dividend payouts in return for the prospect of higher stock values over a longer period. In effect, corporations can retain earnings because their stockholders allow them to retain earnings. If uncertainty clouds the economic scene and if a new market structure makes stock investment an increasingly hazardous undertaking for individuals, then investors will demand a much larger share of those earnings in the form of dividends—and corporate issuers will be forced to shoulder much heavier burdens of external financing. From the corporate point of view, this is—or should be—the starting point for understanding what investor confidence in the securities markets is all about.

The uncertainty and disillusionment which characterize our national state of mind today have spilled over into the economic area and prompted a great many searching questions but, by and large, I believe the American people still trust the national economy. Despite the unmistakable and understandable sounds of frustration we've been hearing with increasing frequency, I believe that most people still have faith in the ability of our great financial institutions—including the stock market—to serve the national interest.

It is a fact that in 1973—a year shot through with international economic and political upheavals, rampant domestic inflation, and an unprecedented crisis of public confidence in the integrity of government—the U.S. economy did not perform at all badly. With the notable and widely publicized exception of the securities industry, which posted an aggregate pre-tax loss of $50 million in 1973, American business enjoyed a profitable year.

Sounds of Upheaval

Many commentators have attributed the securities industry losses—which ran into hundreds of millions of dollars earlier in the year—to public uncertainty and dissatisfaction with the course of national and international events. Most analyses, however, tend to overlook another very important factor that has not been measured: public awareness that powerful forces are at work to bring about necessary and perhaps dramatic changes in the way brokers do business.

Elkins Wetherill, President.
PBW Stock Exchange
Philadelphia, Baltimore, Washington

The sounds of upheaval in our industry have not exactly been muted. A long, and sometimes acrimonious, debate has welled up from the near-calamitous securities industry paper work and financial crises of 1967-1970, focusing on complex, far-reaching proposals to drastically restructure the industry and revolutionize its operations. I find it impossible to assume—as many people seem to have done—that the public is unaware that tremendously important changes are on the way. It seems much more likely that the public misunderstands what is due to happen or, worse, that there is a nationwide failure to grasp what the prospective changes portend for millions of individual investors and for the future economic well-being of this country.

It may be regrettable that large numbers of investors have adopted a wait-and-see attitude. But under the circumstances, it should not be surprising.

The Corporate Lament

What is surprising is the puzzlement with which many corporate executives view the current lack of public enthusiasm for their companies' securities. The typical lament goes something like this:

"I don't understand it. We've had a great year (or two or three great years in succession). Sales are booming. We're expanding at a faster rate than ever before. I had to go over our profit figures myself to make certain they weren't exaggerated. Our prospects for both the short and long range are fantastic. But our stock is selling at only 10 (or 8 or 6) times earnings. Nobody wants it. The institutions are walking along the top tier, making love to 50 or 100 issues and trampling the rest of us into the ground, while the individual investor either flirts with yield-oriented investments or just sits on his savings and twiddles his thumbs. With our stock selling below book value, it would be suicidal for us to go out and raise equity capital—and with interest rates going right through the roof, we'd have to be crazy to borrow. So here we are, patting ourselves on the back with one hand and throwing the other hand up in despair. The only consolation is that our competitors' balance sheets are almost as good as ours, and they don't seem any better off than we are."

According to many corporate executives the chief villain in this picture is The Institution—a composite dominating market force that refuses to recognize that thousands of progressive, well-managed companies are doing a really fine job, and somehow manages to prevent everyone else from recognizing it, too.

This is not the place to debate whether or not that's a fair judgment. But it is pertinent to observe that, generically, the large financial institution—insurance companies, pension funds and other big investors—has become the favorite whipping-boy of frustrated prosperity.

9

On the one hand, thousands of corporate executives seem understandably disturbed that institutional activity is heavily concentrated in the stocks of a relative handful of fortunate corporate giants. And on the other, the voice of the individual investor rings out loud and clear that because of their tremendous financial clout, the "big guys"—the institutions—receive favored treatment from brokers.

Neither allegation is entirely without validity. Institutions have heavy fiduciary responsibilities which can make it very logical for them to cluster in the vicinity of proven long-term success or super-attractive prospects. And brokers can hardly be faulted for being pleased to do business with financially strong customers.

The Colossus Theory

Unfortunately, somewhere along the line, facts and logic seem to have cohabited with frustration and resentment to produce a mystique of disgruntlement called "institutional domination of the market." This holds, in its most extreme form, that most of us will live to see and rue the day when 25 or 50 gigantic institutions effectively control the bulk of American business.

It could happen. In twentieth-century economics, "impossible" is a word to be handled very gingerly. But almost anything of that scope can be avoided—or so we must hope—by a few intelligently conceived precautions.

The colossus theory begins innocently enough with the observation that institutional activity in the market has been increasing by leaps and bounds. But it follows through with the sly non sequitur that the individual investor is being squeezed out of the market by a combination of institutional muscle and securities industry neglect. From there it just takes a bit of fancy footwork to reach the conclusion that all the rejected individual investors will, in self-defense, immerse themselves in insurance companies, pension funds, mutual funds and the like—until everybody qualifies as a nameless, faceless particle of an institution.

Inevitable? Not quite.

The Individual Investor Lives

Despite the present high ratio of institutional to individual participation in the market, it's much too early to write the individual investor's obituary. Consider a few relevant, but not very widely recognized facts and figures.

Back in 1961, the individual investor was the acknowledged hub of the securities marketplace— sought after, cultivated, wooed, beloved of brokers and corporations. In that year, individuals accounted for 61% of the value of public trading on the New York Stock Exchange, i.e., all trading other than that of Exchange members for their own accounts—and 67% of public share volume. The remainder—39% of dollar value and 33% of volume—

11

was done by institutions. Average daily volume on the Exchange that year was 4.1 million shares.

During the next decade, a new national economic hero emerged. The financial institution, ready, able and eager to pour fabulous sums into the stock market, found itself besieged by brokers and corporate suitors. The tempo of the marketplace changed almost overnight. By the first half of 1971 the relative proportions of institutional and individual activity had more than reversed. Individuals now accounted for only 32% of the value of public trading and 40% of volume, while the institutional segments soared to 68% and 60%, respectively. But—and it's a very significant *but*—average daily volume had skyrocketed to nearly 17 million shares over the same period.

The proportions are probably about the same today, plus or minus a percentage point or two. It doesn't require great mathematical skill to recognize that while individuals now account for a much smaller part of the total trading pie, the pie itself has grown enormously.

In terms of the numbers of shares traded, it is true enough that institutional participation increased eightfold over that decade. It is no less true that individual participation nearly tripled—from a daily average of 1.9 million shares in 1961 to a daily average of 5.3 million shares in 1971. Similarly, the dollar value of institutional trading has increased tremendously—but the dollar value of individual trading has also increased, albeit at a much slower rate.

To paraphrase Mark Twain's famous cable to the Associated Press, the demise of the individual investor has been greatly exaggerated.

Institutional Activity Will Top Out

But what about the institutional investor?

There are growing signs that the rush of institutional activity that created the present imbalance between individual and institutional participation in the market may be losing some steam.

It now seems likely that over the next five years, the growth of institutional activity will gradually decelerate, topping out short of an 80% market share measured by the dollar value of public trading, before 1980.

Let me say it first: a range of 70-80% for institutional trading is not to be lightly dismissed. But in view of some of the more flamboyant predictions of the recent past, it is not alarming either—especially when linked with the likelihood that total trading activity will continue to increase substantially. Moreover, since, as we are constantly reminded, institutional activity normally is concentrated in higher-priced stocks, we would expect that activity to account for a lesser proportion of share volume.

My belief that institutional trading is due to peak out is based on three major factors.

First, we can anticipate a slowdown in the growth of institutional assets, strongly influenced by a leveling off of pension fund assets—the largest single source of institutional investment funds—as an increasing number of plans begin to reach maturity.

Second, the percentage of institutional assets invested in equities is also on the road to leveling off. It became fashionable in the 1960's for institutions —particularly pension funds—to aim for a 50% allocation of assets to stock holdings. Since many institutions started the '60s well below that level, a strenuous effort of active investment was often exerted to achieve it. With the proportion of assets invested in equities now at or near the desired level in many institutions, it seems reasonable to anticipate a slower growth rate in the years ahead.

A third—and critical—factor in determining institutional activity is the turnover rate of existing portfolios. During the 1960s and early 70s, aggressive competition among institutions to attract investment assets led to a fundamental change in institutional investment strategy—to the emphasis on so-called portfolio "performance" achieved through frequent trading.

As a number of corporate executives have noted with dismay, some of the glamor attached to portfolio performance has begun to wear thin. Some slowing of allegedly excessive institutional turnover rates has been identified over the past three years. It does not seem unreasonable to assume some further leveling and perhaps even a decline in institutional turnover rates in the years ahead.

The Dynamics of Change

Clearly, the institutional phenomenon, whatever course it takes in the years ahead, has left an indelible imprint on the character of the U.S. securities markets. Within the space of a dozen years, soaring activity has brought unprecedented growth to the securities industry itself, and disaster to those who could not keep up with the dizzying change of pace. Computer technology hit Wall Street like a comet in the early 1960's. By the early 1970's, we had cleared away the debris of the impact, unsnarled a monumental paperwork jam, survived two major industry-wide recessions, and learned to harness the computer's capabilities to the unique needs of a two-century-old business.

Today, we are pushing on to develop new ways to put this technology to work for both the industry and the public—speeding the transmission of orders and market data, revolutionizing the securities-handling processes that nearly strangled an entire industry, and looking ahead to a vast communications linkage of securities markets that may ultimately girdle the globe.

The stage is now being set for the most dramatic changes of all: changes in the basic structure of the securities industry, changes that will determine the future of the U.S. capital markets.

The question facing us is whether these changes

will be convulsive or orderly, and whether the fundamental strengths of the U.S. capital markets system will survive the necessary lengthy period of transition into which we will soon propel ourselves.

These are tough questions to which there are no easy answers. Some of the best minds in the country have been grappling with them for several years. Securities industry leaders, knowledgeable members of Congress, the Federal regulatory authorities, the nation's top economic experts, and a host of informed and uninformed commentators from all walks of life have contributed to the debate that will ultimately shape a guiding national policy.

Inexplicably, the one major element of the economy that stands to gain or lose the most—depending upon whether the securities industry is properly or improperly restructured — seems to have remained outside the discussion, unaware of the issues.

On the basis of the evidence to date, it would be easy to conclude that the majority of the corporate community simply doesn't see any reason to get involved.

To be sure, there are exceptions. Many of the corporate leaders who are Public Directors of the New York and American Stock Exchanges have been working at the heart of the issues from the very beginning. The Committee of Publicly Owned Companies has been addressing some specific problems. But I cannot understand—and I frankly deplore—the apparent disinclination of the bulk of Corporate America to get involved, to contribute its vast resources of expertise, to know what it thinks, and to articulate its views in the forum of the on-going public policy debate.

From where I sit, the real threat to corporate growth today does not come from foreign competition, or from spiraling production and distribution costs, or from government encroachment on the traditional freedom of private enterprise. The real threat to corporate growth today comes from corporate reluctance to demand a role in determining the future structure and operations of the markets where corporate securities are traded and evaluated.

That will be read as a harsh comment and I do not expect it to be received gladly. But in all good conscience, I can temper it only by adding that nothing would please me more than to find that I have to retract it.

profits in all directions. Everybody seemed to be in the market. Everybody had a favorite profit story to tell. Publicly owned corporations were expanding in all directions. Brokerage firms were opening new offices daily. People who had never seen a stock certificate before tossed their savings into the pot and—wonder of wonders—a stream of capital gains poured back at them. Stock Exchange trading floors nearly buckled under the weight of orders pouring in from all over. The institutional boom swung into high gear, with millions of individual investors hanging onto the institutions' coattails. Corporate values soared. On the New York Stock Exchange, original listings of corporate issues reached new peaks; so did mergers and consolidations among companies already listed.

Down in The Street, brokerage firms found themselves wading knee-deep in a rising flood of paper—orders, confirmations, bills, stock certificates, transfer instructions, all the paraphernalia of ways of doing business that had been overtaken by the times. But these were "problems of prosperity," and the industry could afford to hire more people to handle the paperwork while new computers were being installed and taught to do much of the work.

It didn't quite pan out that way. The new people were inexperienced and the new computers were slow learners. Firms that were knee-deep in paperwork at the beginning of 1968 were up to their necks by the end of the year.

A Major Financial Crisis

The following year, 1969, proved to be a critical turning point. Bit by bit, the paperwork began to yield to a massive industry-wide corrective effort— sparked by, among other things, round-the-clock implementation of an Exchange automated securities depository system to immobilize stock certificates and aided somewhat by a slight cooling off of the nationwide investment fever. At first, the industry actually welcomed the lower volume level which simplified the final push to dry up the remains of the paperwork flood.

By May 1969, although no one knew it then, the boom was over. While volume began to ease off very slightly, stock prices suffered dramatic reversals and the value of securities inventories began dropping sharply. Thus, while the level of business remained deceptively high, many brokerage firms began experiencing serious financial difficulties. As the reversal gathered momentum, firms which had made huge financial commitments for automation and other back-office improvements—as well as for expanded capacity to meet the earlier demands for customer service—found their profit margins dwindling and then turning into losses.

Over the full year 1969, 83% of the common stocks listed on the New York Stock Exchange declined in value. By contrast, in 1967, 86% of listed common stocks had risen in value—most of them very substantially—and, in 1968, 79% had moved upward. Significantly, while the volume of shares traded dipped only fractionally from 1968 to 1969, the *value* of shares traded dropped from $145 billion to $130 billion. And while volume in 1970 remained high—largely due to a fourth-quarter rally —the value of shares traded plunged to $103 billion —a decline of almost 30% over two years.

What followed in the securities industry was a financial crisis of epic dimensions. When the dust finally settled, more than 160 New York Stock Exchange member firms—and an undisclosed but presumably as large a number of non-NYSE brokerage firms — were out of business. Public attention focused on the New York Stock Exchange's efforts to assist the public customers of 17 of the firms that were hardest hit by the crisis. In a move unparalleled in the annals of U.S. business, member firms that survived the financial holocaust authorized the Exchange to ante up as much as $140 million of their money, if necessary, to shield the public customers of their former competitors from financial disaster. That action, by shoring up public confidence in the fundamental integrity of the U.S. securities industry, probably saved the industry from total collapse and, thus, averted a national economic disaster.

With the spotlight today on other crisis-afflicted industries, people tend to forget that when the chips were down, the brokerage community put its money where its responsibility to the public was. And just three years after the fact, it seems no more than a footnote to one of the most incredible dramas in U.S. economic history that most of the $140 million has been spent and little, if any, of it will ever be recouped.

The Role of the Auction Market

A lot of people have learned a lot of lessons from the experiences of 1967-1970. But to my mind, one stark, simple fact rises almost unrecognized by the American business community or by government from those experiences:

Throughout the boom and bust, throughout the series of operational and financial crises, throughout the convulsive changes that rocked the securities industry and the entire business community, the securities auction markets continued to function relatively smoothly.

Millions of orders to buy and sell listed securities poured into the market. Bids to buy and offers to sell continued to meet in a two-way auction to produce the best available price for both the buyer and the seller at a given moment. The forces of supply and demand, constantly interacting in the auction crowds of brokers on the stock exchange trading floors, continued to evaluate and determine the prices—sometimes rising, sometimes falling, sometimes remaining unchanged—of the stocks of the world's major corporate enterprises, and continued to keep those price changes orderly. The corporations themselves may not always have been pleased by the effects of supply and demand on the value of their stocks—but they always knew, as they know today, what those effects were and how the investing public, individuals and institutions alike, were reacting to economic factors such as inflation and changing interest rates; and how the public regarded what corporate management was accomplishing or failing to accomplish. In terms of clarity, certainty and breadth of judgment, capitalist ingenuity has produced no more accurate method of assessing corporate performance — within the limits of a particular economic environment—than the auction market pricing system.

Paul Kolton, Chairman;
Richard M. Burdge, President.
American Stock Exchange

24

ma
a

th
fluen...   ...re-
fore, exert   ...ess of
corporations   ...rs to buy.
They help determin...   ...and growing
companies to raise capital, a... ...asoned companies to innovate and expand.

Thus, in the final analysis, the securities auction markets, by accurately determining the prices of corporate stocks, play a key role in the allocation of capital—significantly influencing the growth, stability and productivity of the national economy.

Underlying that key role is the uniquely American phenomenon of a broad base of individual public shareownership which aims at providing the widest possible dispersion of investment decisions. Those decisions, flowing to a central marketplace in a constant stream of orders to buy and sell stocks, are essential to maintaining fair, orderly, continuous markets, in depth, in the stocks of hundreds of the world's largest corporations. These highly liquid markets, in which the forces of supply and demand constantly interact to produce minimal price changes from one transaction to the next, fulfill the key role in the continuous evaluation of corporate performance that is the fundamental strength of the U.S. capital markets system.

Experience has shown conclusively that it is only when the basic investment decisions are widely shared—when economic power is distributed among literally millions of decision-makers—that the U.S. capital markets and the U.S. economy can perform most effectively.

Our recognition of the key role played by millions of individual investors in helping maintain strong U.S. capital markets explains why, at the New York Stock Exchange, we have been so deeply concerned by persistent public reluctance to participate more fully in the market.

Shareowners' Gripes

At the beginning of 1973, we estimated that, for the first time in nearly a generation, there had been a one-year net decline in the total number of U.S. shareowners. It has been widely assumed that additional investors have joined the ranks of the 800,000 who disappeared during 1972. We expect to have some new data in the very near future that will indicate whether this was indeed the case.

There has been no dearth of explanations—informed or otherwise—of why, in a period of fairly general national prosperity, many investors were locking up their portfolios, shunning their brokers, and pointedly ignoring hundreds of attractive investment opportunities.

John P. Guerin, Jr., Chairman of the
Board; Thomas P. Phelan, President.
Pacific Stock Exchange, Inc.

To obtain first-hand answers, the Exchange invited a nationwide cross-section of more than 1200 small individual investors and potential investors to sound off and let us know their gripes. We asked for candor, and we got it.

We uncovered lingering memories of the unpleasant experiences of 1969-70, and an uneasy feeling that it might all happen again—that brokerage firms might be vulnerable to a recurrence of paperwork problems and financial difficulties.

Similarly, our survey confirmed the belief that widespread public confusion, brought on by unsettling economic and political developments at home and abroad, has led many people to divert their investable funds into other channels.

It also became clear that many investors were put off by their awareness of the scope of institutional activity in the market, and by their feeling that the U.S. securities industry has come to favor the mysterious "big guys."

Running through investors' comments—as a constant or recurring theme — was the feeling that brokers simply no longer cared to have small individual investors as customers.

Whether these views are valid or not—and whether or not they add up to a "crisis" of investor confidence, as some commentators claim—is really beside the point. The mere fact that they are widely held and reflect a substantial *lack* of public confidence in the market is reason enough for serious concern.

At the same time, not all the investor reactions called for sackcloth and ashes. We also found, somewhat contradictorily but encouragingly, that these investors generally continue to regard corporate stocks as good investment vehicles; that they regard brokers as trustworthy professionals; and, perhaps most significant, that they are not at all eager to change the basic broker-client personal relationship that has evolved over the years.

All in all, the comments added up to a firm call for reassurance—not just in words, but in deeds that will merit public confidence.

I feel strongly that it is not only wrong to try to buy confidence with empty phrases — it's stupid.

Nor do you stimulate confidence by wringing your hands and blaming everything on the other fellow. You *earn* confidence. You earn it by facing and evaluating problems, and by finding the best ways of solving them.

Putting Our House in Order

That's what we've been trying to do at the New York Stock Exchange. First and most important, we've devoted a major effort to setting our own house in order to guard against any possible recurrence of past crises—both in terms of substantially stronger capital requirements for member firms, and in terms of operational capability. Some measure of the success of these efforts may be judged from the fact that in 1968, at the height of the operational crisis, average daily volume on the Exchange was less than 13 million shares; today, Exchange and member firm facilities are handling 16-million-share averages without strain, as a matter of routine.

Equally important, we are doing everything we can to make investing as genuinely attractive to as many people as possible. Our programs range from strengthening the Exchange's market-making and service facilities, to specific efforts to obtain more equitable tax treatment for investors.

And let me be the very first to acknowledge that our motives are not entirely altruistic. It would be less than accurate to say merely that we want millions of individual investors to participate in the market. If the market is going to function at full capacity and effectiveness—and if it is going to fulfill its crucial role in stimulating dynamic national economic growth—then we *need* the participation of millions of individual investors, no less than we need the participation of large institutional investors.

The U.S. capital markets need the breadth of decision-making and the steady stream of buy and sell orders that only millions of individual investors can provide. Our capital markets also need the tremendous financial resources that only the great institutions can supply. It isn't a question of either/or. We must have both.

It has been alleged that the institutions fueled the 1968-69 market boom and, therefore, were also responsible, at least indirectly, for many of the unpleasant consequences that followed. It has also been claimed that, during the worst years, the institutions were in the market when nobody else was, that they saved the market from disintegrating and, therefore, have earned the right to dominate it.

I find all such allegations boring and unproductive. I believe the time has come to abandon the fiction that there must be an inherent, unavoidable conflict between the interests of institutional and individual investors. It is far more essential to concentrate on developing a market system that can serve the legitimate needs of corporate issuers and, at the same time, properly and efficiently accommodate every investor—large or small—who seeks no more than the opportunity to participate fairly in this country's economic growth.

The problems we have experienced in the recent past tend to obscure the fact that this nation has the strongest, most liquid and, yes, most efficient, capital markets in the world. The fact that most of America takes them for granted is ample enough proof of that. If, at the same time, there isn't room enough for everyone who wants to participate fairly in those markets, then something is very seriously wrong with the system. And the first objective of any effort to restructure the system should be to improve and strengthen it and to assure beyond any possible doubt that the opportunity to participate is readily available to anyone who seeks it.

Ernest Muth, President.
Intermountain Stock Exchange
Salt Lake City

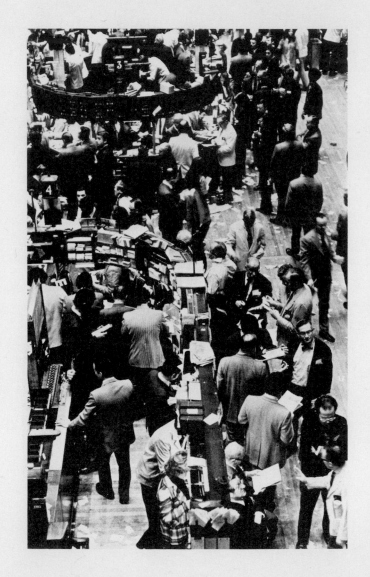

TOWARD A NATIONAL MARKET SYSTEM

In the aftermath of the traumatic securities industry paperwork and financial crises, Congress set itself the monumental task of determining what might be done, legislatively, to prevent the possibility of comparable future calamities.

With urgent support from the industry, the Securities Investor Protection Act was passed and signed into law at the end of 1970. This legislation created the Federally chartered Securities Investor Protection Corporation (SIPC) to provide an important measure of protection for public investors' funds and securities in the event of the failure of a brokerage firm with which they do business.

But this was really an emergency measure, sparked by the realization that an industry in the midst of an intense financial crisis had already promised to shell out as much as $140 million to protect the customers of brokerage firms in liquidation, and might be literally unable to support the immediate costs of another major failure. The industry was willing to underwrite SIPC through a specific schedule of assessment-contributions, but at the end of 1970, the key feature of the legislation was that it provided for a $1 billion line of credit from the U.S. Treasury for use when and if SIPC's own industry-contributed funds should prove inadequate to meet customer protection needs.

The concept has the full support of the New York Stock Exchange and, as far as I know, the Regional exchanges and the full securities industry. The trouble is, the concept is not much closer to becoming a reality today than it was in May 1971—even though the National Securities Market System Act has been reported out by Senator Williams' Subcommittee on Securities to its parent Senate Committee on Banking, Housing and Urban Affairs and could conceivably move much closer to enactment while these pages are being printed.

Senator Williams introduced the Bill on the floor of the Senate on October 2, 1973. Its objectives, as he stated them at that time, are unassailable:

"First, the maintenance of stable and orderly markets with maximum capacity for absorbing trading imbalances without undue price movements. And second, centralization of all buying and selling interests with appropriate protection of public orders. In this way every investor will be assured of receiving the best possible execution of his order, regardless of where it originates."

Thus, the pending legislation mandates the creation of a national market system and makes clear what it is designed to accomplish. It does not offer any precise, detailed description of how the system would work, nor does it present a specific timetable for the system's creation.

At this moment, therefore, no one—not Congress, not the SEC, and certainly not the securities industry itself—can offer a clear picture of what a national market system is going to look like, or when it will actually start functioning. For while the basic technology needed to create the system undoubtedly exists, it has yet to be harnessed to the job. Perhaps most important, it has never been made clear just who is going to foot the bill, which could easily top $100 million.

This is not, in itself, cause for great alarm. You must begin with an idea and then carefully work out the mechanics of implementing it.

The immediate problem that is cause for very deep concern springs from the imminent implementation of an economic concept that is not directly related to the creation of a national market system. This is the decision by the Securities and Exchange Commission—endorsed by both Senator Williams and Representative Moss—to eliminate fixed commission rates on all securities transactions after April 30, 1975.

The desirability of ending fixed commission rates may be debatable. Its inevitability is not. The New York Stock Exchange has not opposed the step.

The Real Danger: Diversion of Order Flow

Just why, then, is the securities industry almost unanimously alarmed? What is the real cause of our anguish?

Simply this: The changeover to a new rate system that mandates competition on the basis of price as well as service will bring sweeping economic changes to the industry. So far so good. These changes *can* be managed in a way that will improve the financial health and efficiency of the industry. But two unavoidable consequences must be acknowledged and integrated smoothly into the overall plan.

First, the end of fixed rates will tend to make the concept of membership on stock exchanges economically irrelevant. Any nonmember broker will be able to negotiate his own access to the exchange markets as a matter of routine.

Francis C. Farwell, Chairman;
Michael E. Tobin, President.
Midwest Stock Exchange, Chicago, Ill.

Second, the pressures of price competition will impel all brokerage firms to concentrate on the most profitable aspects of their business.

We believe these two factors point clearly to one result: a proliferation of dealer markets in exchange-listed securities. As large brokerage firms face spiraling costs and intense price competition, they will find, in many cases, that their survival will depend upon their ability to capitalize on the most readily available profit potential. Virtually every firm will have to re-evaluate its fundamental business mix and operating structure. There will, of course, be powerful inducements to cut costs to the bone. There will also be compelling reasons to de-emphasize all of the marginally profitable activities including, in many instances, stock exchange business in listed securities, which is based on brokerage commissions.

Inevitably, major firms will have to take a close look at the merits of abandoning their roles as broker-agents for securities customers, leaving the exchanges and conducting dealer markets—buying directly from and selling directly to individual investors and institutions—primarily in high-volume listed stocks.

Four of the largest New York Stock Exchange member firms have already declared publicly that they will have to seriously consider quitting the exchanges when competitive rates become effective, unless appropriate offsetting measures are adopted.

Obviously, securities firms must take the best course indicated by the economic pressures exerted on them. Unfortunately, the advantages of switching over to a dealer operation are, for large firms, obvious enough.

As dealers, they will be able to match the flow of orders coming into their offices to in-house inventories in those stocks, picking up the dealer's profit on each transaction. When they find it necessary or desirable to act as agents, they will simply direct orders to the exchanges, negotiating access through one of the remaining member firms.

Moreover, where the flow of orders through a firm is heavy enough, it would be possible, in many instances, to cross orders away from the exchanges and collect the dealer's turn on both sides of a transaction. This might in many instances prove to be greater than a broker's commission on an equivalent transaction. We would not expect a dealer to have difficulty in honoring his fiduciary responsibilities to customers since it would often be possible to match the prevailing quotation spread—or even to improve on it—for both the buyer and the seller. For example, if the best bid in a stock is 50 and the best offer is 50¼, the dealer could cross the orders at 50⅛, pocketing a ⅛-point profit on both sides and still satisfying his obligation to both customers. Of course, in all such instances, the customers of brokers on the exchange trading floors would be excluded. They would have no opportunity to participate in the transaction without dealer intervention, and they would have no way of knowing that a transaction had actually taken place at 50⅛.

This type of perfectly legitimate dealing would be most likely to occur, of course, in the most actively traded stocks. In this connection, it is well worth noting that, in 1972, the 250 most active New York Stock Exchange listed stocks—representing only 15% of the total list—accounted for 51% of reported share volume on the Exchange. In the same year, 16 of some 450 NYSE member firms dealing with the public handled 50% of all agency transactions in listed stocks on our trading floor—and 63 firms handled 75% of all agency transactions.

We are talking here about a flow of some 100,000 orders a day—including market orders and limit orders (those executed when and if a specified price is reached) on both sides of public round-lot and odd-lot transactions—to the floor of the New York Stock Exchange. This is the critical source of supply and demand that enables the securities auction pricing system to operate efficiently today.

In 1973, this flow of orders was translated into average daily volume of more than 16 million shares. Obviously, a decision by a relative handful of large brokerage firms to set up shop as dealers in listed securities would have a tremendous impact that could conceivably shatter the exchange specialist systems.

A diminished flow of orders in specialty stocks

would simultaneously increase the volatility of exchange markets and encourage specialists to move off the exchange so they, too, could compete as "upstairs" dealers and market-makers. Specialists who elected to remain on the exchange floors would still have the fundamental obligation to make continuous markets in their assigned stocks—while their "upstairs" competitors could concentrate on making markets in stocks of their own choosing and under whatever conditions they might find most congenial and advantageous to themselves. Moreover, the economic incentives for specialists to make closer markets would decline as the flow of orders on which they now earn a part of the agency commis-

Vincent M. Cantella, Chairman;
James E. Dowd, President.
Boston Stock Exchange

sion dries up. And as specialists' quotations widen, "upstairs" market-makers would find it easy to siphon still more business away from the auction markets, while still preserving the illusion of trading within price spreads set in the auction process on the exchange trading floors.

Our urgent concern, in a nutshell, is that while we are all waiting for a national market system to begin operating, the existing auction markets will be fragmented and distorted to an extent that will stubbornly resist any subsequent legislative or administrative efforts to restore their health and viability. And the impact on the auction markets will intensify as the transitional period lengthens. Any realistic appraisal of progress thus far, combined with the formidable array of legislative, administrative and technological problems which must be resolved before a national market system efficiently reports its first trade—and the existing timetable for the changeover to competitive rates — leaves very little room for optimism.

The Principal Losers

But even if the stock exchanges do wither during the interim period, that will be by no means the most important or most dangerous consequence.

What matters most is that the principal losers from a proliferation of dealer markets in listed securities will be the issuing corporations and millions of individual investors.

Corporate issuers would be deprived, to a large extent, of the existing clarity and certainty—now taken for granted by most corporate executives—of the auction pricing mechanism. They would be confronted instead with a maze of dealer pricing decisions. Sources of trading would be difficult, perhaps impossible, to identify. By acting as dealers, rather than as agents, major handlers of securities transactions would acquire the freedom—now denied to exchange specialists—to refuse to make markets when the going gets rough. Regulating a sprawling dealer market would be vastly complicated not only by the physical dispersion of the markets, but also by varying prices and quality of the markets from one independent market-maker to the next.

Thus, by fragmenting the listed securities markets, a dealer-oriented system would, in fact, give corporate issuers no choice but to accept less disciplined evaluation and trading of their securities.

The implications for public investors are no more encouraging.

A truncated auction market, seeing only a fraction of the present order flow in listed stocks, would inevitably lose depth and liquidity. Individual investors, hoping to circumvent impaired price continuity in the auction market, might turn to the dealers—and find that their worst fears are realized, that the dealers really would rather cater to big institutions and will offer prices on listed stocks to individuals strictly on a take-it-or-leave-it basis.

Widespread uncertainty and dissatisfaction with their treatment in a dealer-oriented system could lead millions of individual investors to lose confidence in our markets and withdraw from active participation in them.

If individuals came to feel less welcome as active buyers and sellers of stocks already outstanding they probably would also draw back from participating in new issues of corporate stocks. Thus companies seeking to raise venture capital through new equity issues would find themselves shut off from an important source of investment funds and would have to rely more and more heavily on institutions to provide capital for expansion. It seems likely that faced with the alternative of burgeoning institutional influence in internal corporate affairs, many managements might opt for more conservative growth policies.

As in Europe, the emphasis in investment could readily shift from the expectation of capital gains to the certainty of dividend payouts.

If this occurred on any substantial scale—and the available evidence certainly points in that direction—issuing corporations would unquestionably find it more difficult to finance modernization and expansion through high levels of retained earnings.

Exit the bright prospect for profitable, peaceful co-existence in the market of individual and institutional investors. Re-enter the spectre of total institutional domination of the American capital markets, in the European fashion, where the markets traditionally have been strongly dealer-oriented.

Historically, the great banking institutions have almost completely dominated the securities markets of Continental Europe, investing and trading heavily among themselves for their own accounts and acting on behalf of a relatively small group of very wealthy sophisticated private investors. Through their massive holdings, the European banks exert effective control over most of the large corporate enterprises in their own countries. The securities markets such as they are have neither sought nor highly regarded individual participation either in the markets or in corporate ownership. As a consequence, the uniquely American phenomena of stock market liquidity, public disclosure of transactions and active direct individual participation in the market, are virtually unknown.

Only recently have our counterparts in Europe begun to consider the merits and advantages of welcoming large numbers of individual investors into the market and attempting to build the type of widespread public participation that characterizes the U.S.—and to a lesser extent the Canadian, British and Japanese—securities markets.

It would be ironic indeed if a European movement toward the U.S. style of capital markets were to coincide with a proliferation of European-style markets in this country.

The ultimate result would almost certainly be to

concentrate the ownership of American business increasingly in the hands of a relatively few enormous investors controlling huge pools of capital.

The Simple Solution

I have outlined a pretty grim scenario. But there is a way—a very simple way—to circumvent it.

The auction valuation process for corporate securities exists today only on the New York, American, PBW, Mid-West, Pacific and other regional stock exchanges. There is no comparable system of trading in the existing over-the-counter dealer markets, nor is it contemplated that an auction process can or will be imposed on the dealer markets with the change over to competitive rates.

Congress and the regulatory authorities have repeatedly stressed the importance of preserving the securities auction markets in any future national securities market system.

At the New York Stock Exchange, we have assumed—and if our assumption is wrong, then *all* bets are off—that it will be possible to build adequate safeguards into such a system. The unresolved issue at this time is how to avoid dismembering the auction markets in the period between the advent of fully competitive commission rates after April 30, 1975 and the establishment of a properly functioning national system at some future unspecified date. The answer, simply and clearly, is to build an effective bridge over the gap.

The Board of Directors of the New York Stock Exchange identified the critical danger as long ago as March 1973—long before the now-pending legislation was written.

The Board called for legislation requiring, concurrently with a changeover to fully competitive rates, that all trading of listed securities take place on registered national securities exchanges.

This proposal has been misinterpreted as meaning that all present over-the-counter dealers in listed stocks—the so-called "third market"—would have to become exchange members. They would not. We believe it should be possible to work out a suitable means of access to the auction market for all bona fide broker-dealers whether members of exchanges or not.

The thrust of the proposal has been misinterpreted as seeking to replace fixed commission rates with another kind of specific economic incentive to membership on stock exchanges. Not so. We have acknowledged that a national market system, which we support, will tend to make stock exchange membership economically irrelevant. And while this separate question will obviously require responsible resolution, it should not be permitted to direct attention away from the key danger of forcing the auction evaluation process itself into obsolescence on the road to a national market system.

Both of these misinterpretations have stirred up a lot of unnecessary dust.

Our proposal would require only that dealers and agents alike—whether exchange members or not — would have to bring their trades in listed stocks to a registered national securities exchange.

This would assure the maximum interplay of public supply and public demand in determining the prices at which listed securities are bought and sold in the public marketplace, and it would increase the amount of market transaction information available to all public investors.

This single, clear, simple requirement would assure the viability of the securities auction markets pending the establishment, with adequate safeguards, of a national securities market system.

The Role of Congress

The final decision that will determine the fate of the U.S. securities auction markets rests with Congress, and with the opinion leaders—elsewhere in government and in the business and academic communities—to whom Congress looks for ideas and guidance.

Fortunately, others have begun to recognize that the serious issues we have raised go far beyond the parochial concerns of the securities industry—that they go straight to the heart of our national economy. At stake are our continuing ability to provide fair and equal access to the nation's listed securities markets for all investors—large and small—and our ability to improve and strengthen the supplies of

A LOOK INTO THE FUTURE

T̲hroughout recorded history, wise men and fools have shared a fascination for trying to predict the future. The securities industry has its share of both —and all of us have tried to get a glimpse into the crystal ball to see the securities market system as it may develop in this country over the next five to ten years.

Although that crystal ball remains somewhat clouded by the uncertain years beyond April 1975, I am hopeful that—with encouragement from Corporate America—Congress will fulfill our hopes for a satisfactory bridge to the future. And beyond that bridge, it is possible to distinguish some provocative shapes and outlines.

I see, essentially, a two-branch national market system, with each branch operating as an independent unit.

One unit will handle all trades in securities not listed on any stock exchange, encompassing, in effect, the present over-the-counter market, and operated by the National Association of Securities Dealers. This market will deal primarily in the stocks of smaller, less-seasoned publicly owned companies which, because of the relatively small numbers of shares outstanding or relatively low levels of share activity, are better-suited to dealer trading than to trading through the auction process.

All elements of this central market for unlisted securities will be linked by a communications network in which the current quotations of every dealer in a particular unlisted issue can be obtained instantaneously, at the flick of a button. This may permit complete automation of all 100-share trades in unlisted stocks; but it seems likely that, at least in the foreseeable future, it will still be necessary to negotiate prices for larger orders by telephone.

The second, much larger and far more complex branch of the national market system will focus exclusively on trading in listed securities. It will be, in effect, a national exchange auction market system, linking the New York, American, PBW, Mid-West, Boston, Pacific, Detroit and other regional stock exchanges into a nationwide—and, ultimately, perhaps—international network.

The two major elements of this network will be a Consolidated Tape and a Computerized Quotation System.

The Consolidated Tape

The Consolidated Tape will report last-sale information on all listed stocks on all exchanges. Actually, the Consolidated Tape will necessarily be *two* tapes, since no single tape could have the capacity to handle all reportable data while keeping pace with market activity. One tape would report all trades in NYSE-listed issues, specifically identifying each trade taking place on another exchange.

The second tape would report all trades in Amex-listed issues plus all trades in all issues listed only on regional exchanges. Here, too, there would be a specific indication of the exchange—other than the Amex, which would presumably account for a majority of the reported trades—on which each trade takes place.

Hal H. Smith, III, President;
M. Edward Denny, Executive Vice President.
Detroit Stock Exchange

Computerized Quotation System

The ultimate configuration of a Computerized Quotation System remains much hazier. It might seem, at first, that it would be relatively simple to design a system similar to that proposed for the unlisted market system, with the major addition of capability for indicating the number of shares behind each bid and offer. However, this could introduce an element of rigidity that might actually diminish the quality of the markets we now have.

A simplified example may help to illustrate the kind of problem that must be solved before a Composite Quotation System can take final shape: a specialist today—on the floor of the New York, American or a Regional stock exchange—may hold and display a bid left with him on behalf of a broker's customer to buy up to 500 shares of a particular stock for, say, 45½. Before that bid is accepted, another broker may enter the auction crowd with a bid of 45⅝ on behalf of *his* customer. The specialist's instructions may permit him to raise his bid immediately to 45¾. If the specialist lacks the split-second ability to change his quote, however, the broker in the crowd may effect a trade with another broker in the crowd at 45⅝. Theoretically, the selling broker would not have obtained the best available price for his customer, and the customer represented by the order held by the specialist would have missed the market.

Thus, the specialist system as it now operates has a measure of flexibility, from which public customers benefit, that might be lost in a more rigidly structured quotation system. Ideally, a new system will apply new levels of technological ingenuity to solve this type of problem and other, still knottier ones. Unfortunately, to date, no one has quite figured out all the answers.

The "Locked-In" Trade

The basic electronic communications linkage among the various participating markets in the national exchange auction market system will make it possible for a customer's order directed to a particular market to be exposed automatically to all public orders already on the books of competing specialists in other markets. This will be accomplished by some form of electronic specialist book—at least for smaller orders which do not require a face-to-face confrontation between the specialist and a floor broker representing a public customer.

Moreover, we look to a completely electronic communications system to achieve the long-sought goal of the "locked-in" trade—where the execution of an order will automatically trigger, in proper sequence, all of the post-trade operations: confirmation, clearing, settlement and transfer of ownership from seller to buyer. The locked-in trade would, in fact, delegate all records-keeping and paperwork to a vast national clearing and depository system which is now being forged from the strongest elements of the various individual systems which have emerged and been continuously refined since the crisis-filled days of 1967-70.

As the crystal ball clears, it is possible to distinguish the forms of investors in San Francisco or New Orleans—or for that matter, in Toronto or Brussels or Melbourne—telephoning orders to their brokers to buy or sell shares of any of the world's major corporations, and learning with absolute certainty—in the time it takes to dictate a letter or boil an egg — that their portfolios have indeed been changed in accordance with their carefully detailed instructions.

The international aspects of what we are trying to achieve are perhaps most exciting of all. For once a national market system is in place and functioning properly, it would be relatively simple to extend the network—by telephone, cable or even communications satellites — to accommodate investors in other countries. This could conceivably extend to linkages among all of the world's major stock exchanges to form an international exchange auction market system, perhaps operating 24 hours a day, serving an international investing public throughout the capitalist world.

But, obviously, before the United States can take the initiative required to establish a global stock exchange system, we must set our own priorities in order.

The National Market System

The vision of a national market system has stimulated many of the finest minds in this country to develop an extraordinarily complex concept into a practical model that will then have to be refined and polished and perfected. However it is not unreasonable to hope that by the end of the present decade—by 1980—a national securities market system will be a working reality.

The only possible hitch that I see—and, as I've tried to indicate, it looms as a whopper—is the sharp and immediate danger that in our national eagerness to change the system, we might just make the critical mistake of destroying the basic elements of the system we are trying to improve.

The *wrong* kind of changes obviously will be harmful to the securities industry. More important, the *wrong* kind of changes can vaporize public confidence in corporate stocks as a viable, direct, personal investment medium and restructure the U.S. securities markets in a completely institutional mold. Perhaps most serious and threatening of all, the *wrong* kind of changes can wreck the fundamental securities evaluation process that Corporate America depends upon, almost instinctively, today, as a firm basis for many of the hard decisions that are ultimately translated into corporate growth and profits.

These are luxuries no nation can afford. They are luxuries that we in the United States, particularly, must deny ourselves if we are to successfully face the staggering investment capital challenges of the immediate future and move forward, more than two hundred million of us, in a growing, prosperous and abundant economic environment.